KW-224-778

Classic
HITS

Exclusive distributors:

International Music Publications Limited
Southend Road, Woodford Green, Essex IG8 8HN
International Music Publications Limited
25 Rue D'Hauteville, 75010 Paris, France
International Music Publications GmbH Germany
Marstallstrasse 8, D-80539 München, Germany
Nuova Carisch S.R.L.
Via M.F. Quintiliano 40, 20138 Milano, Italy
Danmusik
Vognmagergade 7, DK-1120 Copenhagen K, Denmark

Production by Sadie Cook
Choral arrangements by Ned Bennett and Jon Halton
Music processed by MiDiservices
Cover design by xheight design limited

Published 1997

DON'T BE
A MUSIC
COPYCAT!

© International Music Publications Limited
Southend Road, Woodford Green, Essex IG8 8HN, England

4.95

Bohemian Rhapsody

Words and Music by FREDDIE MERCURY
Arranged by Ned Bennett

4

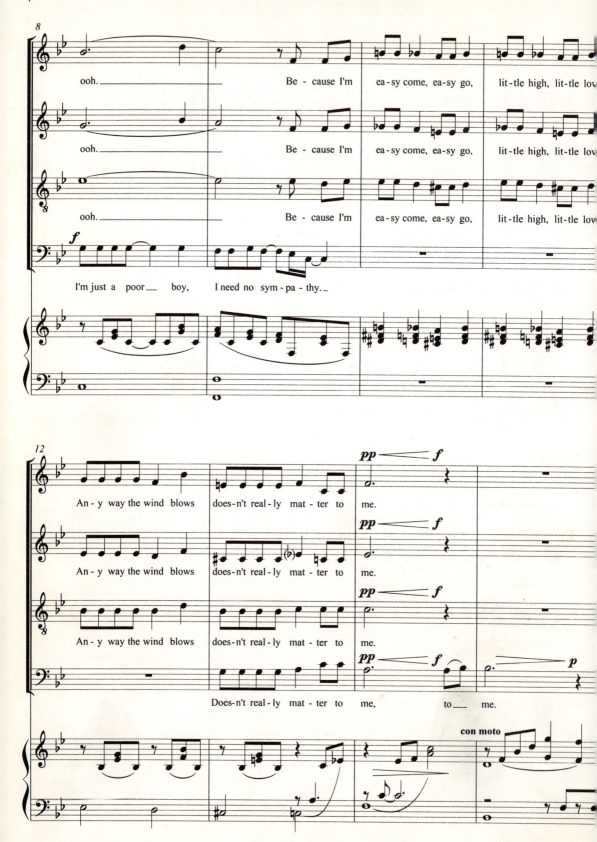

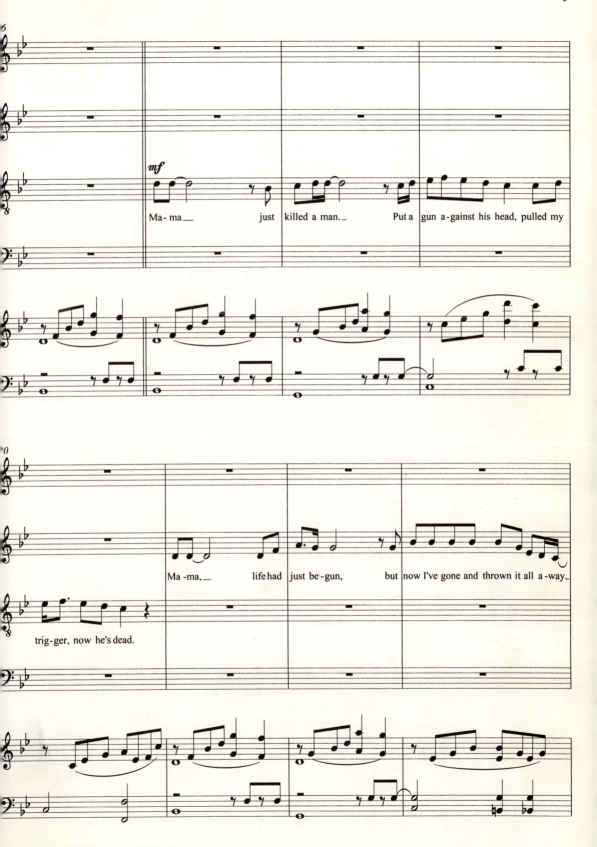

Too late, ___ my time has come, ___ sends

Good-bye, ___ ev-'ry bo- dy, I've got to go, ___ got-ta

Good-bye, ___ ev-'ry bo- dy, I've got to go, ___ got-ta

shiv- ers down my spine, bo-dy's ach-ing all the time. ___

10

14

La Bamba

Adapted by RITCHIE VALENS
Arranged by Jon Halton

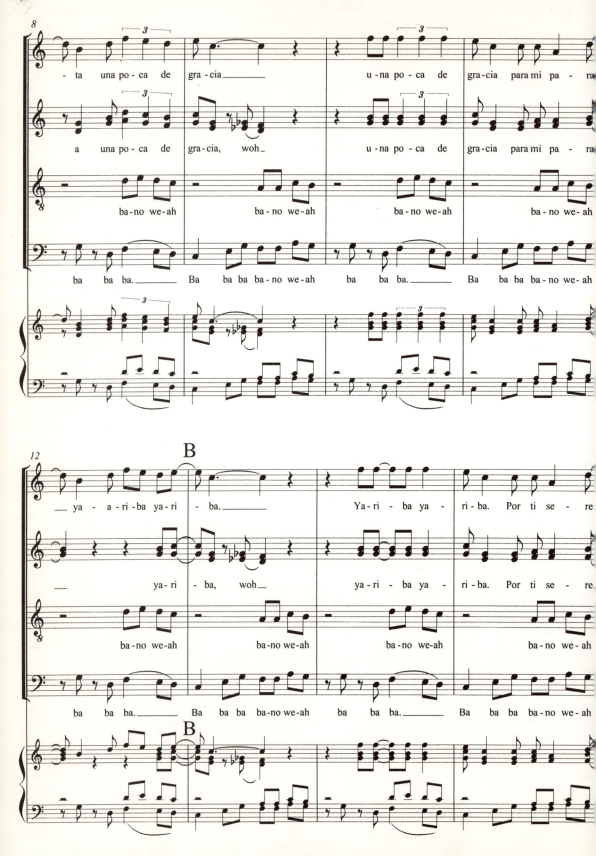

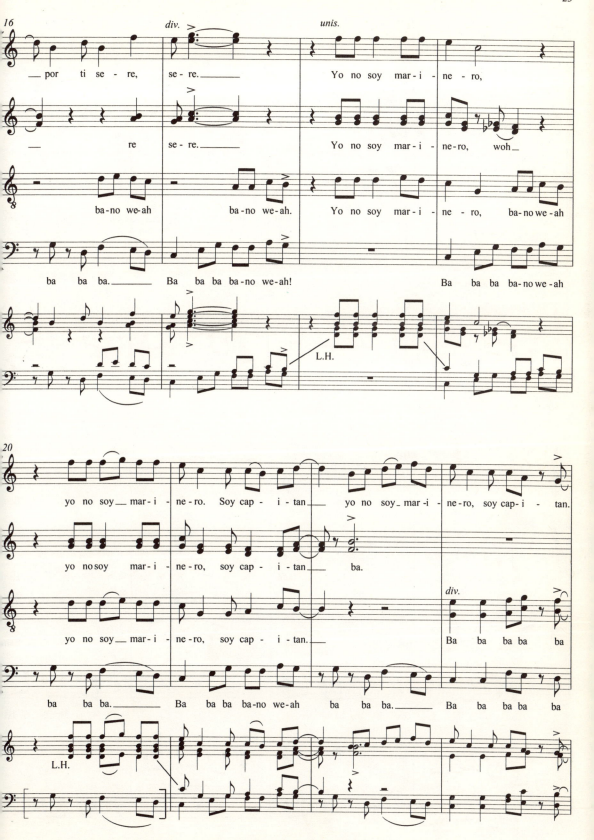

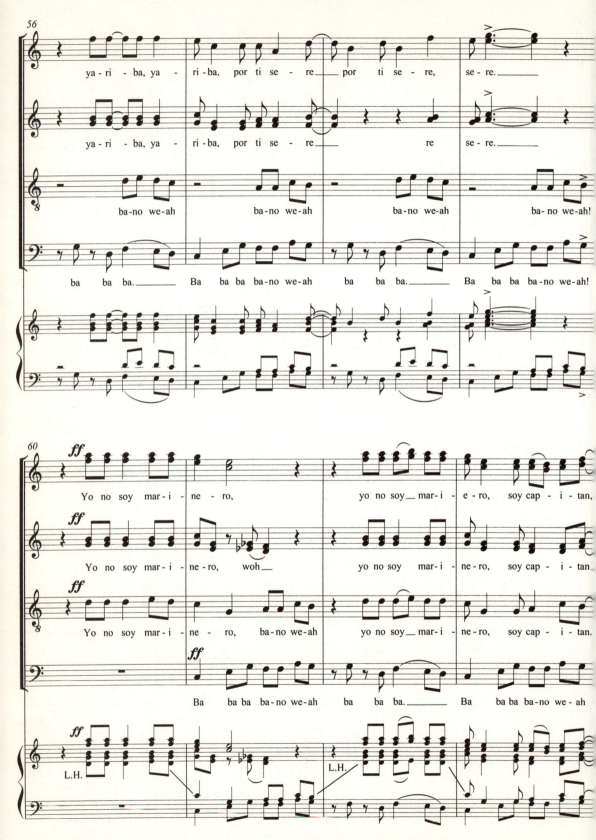

30

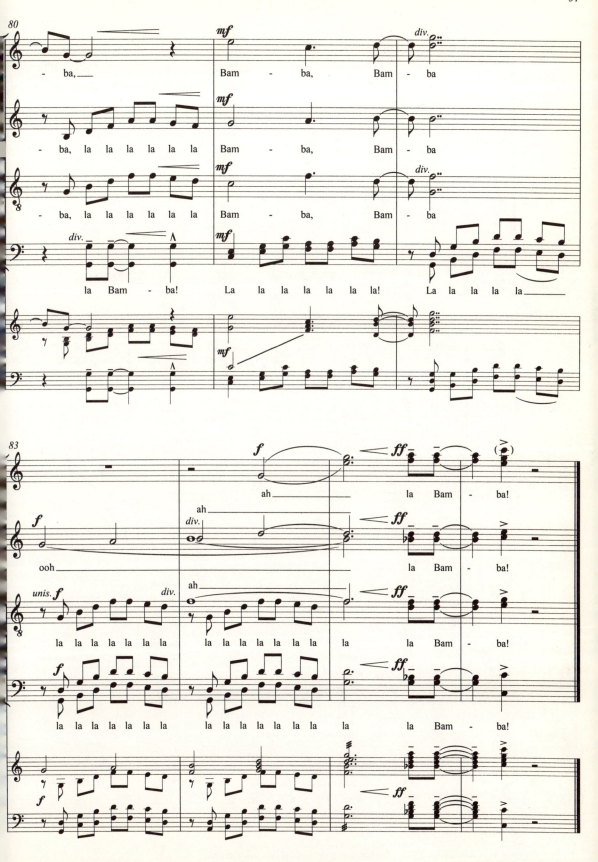

Sacrifice

Words and Music by ELTON JOHN and BERNIE TAUPIN
Arranged by Jon Haltor

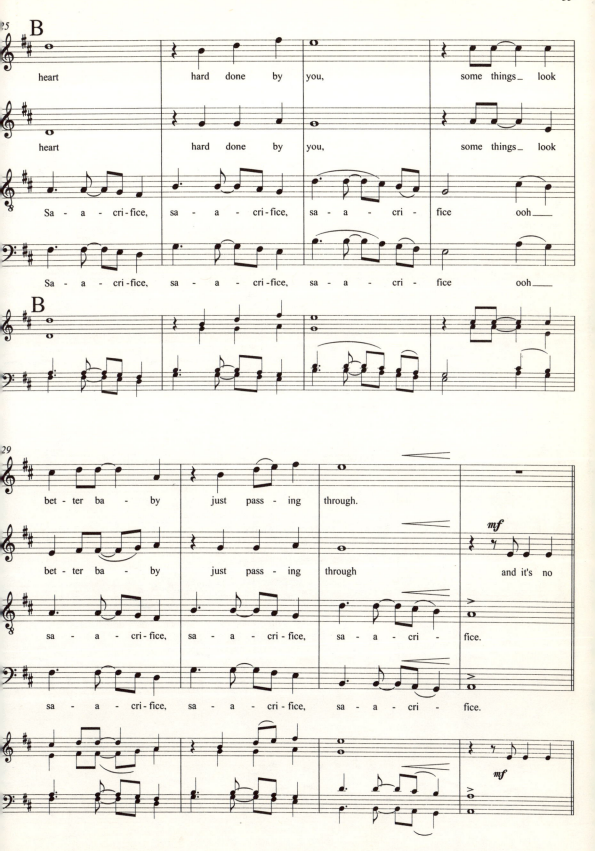

40

A Whiter Shade Of Pale

Words and Music by KEITH REID and GARY BROOK
Arranged by Ned Benr

46

48

Why Do Fools Fall In Love?

Words and Music by FRANKIE LYMON,
HERMAN SANTIAGO and JIMMY MERCHANT
Arranged by Jon Halton

* Should be pronounced as in the title of the song.

50

* Should be pronounced as in the title of the song.

52

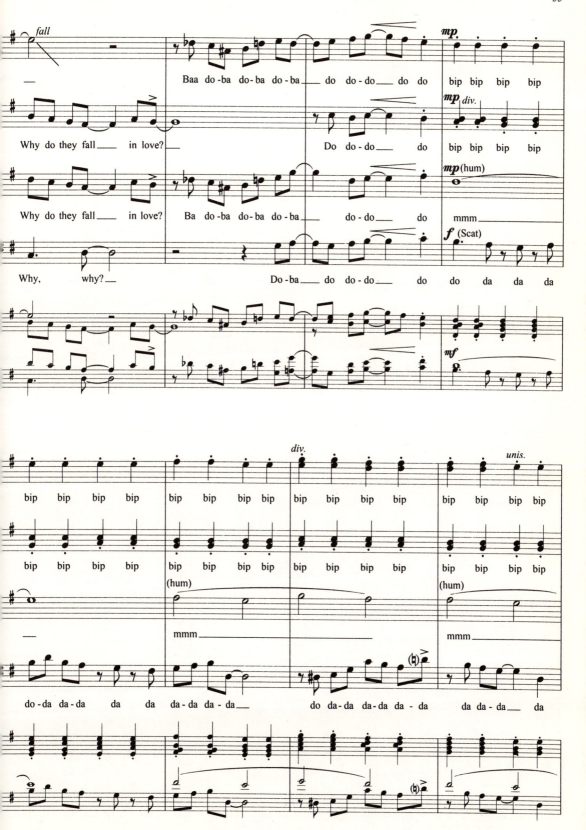

58

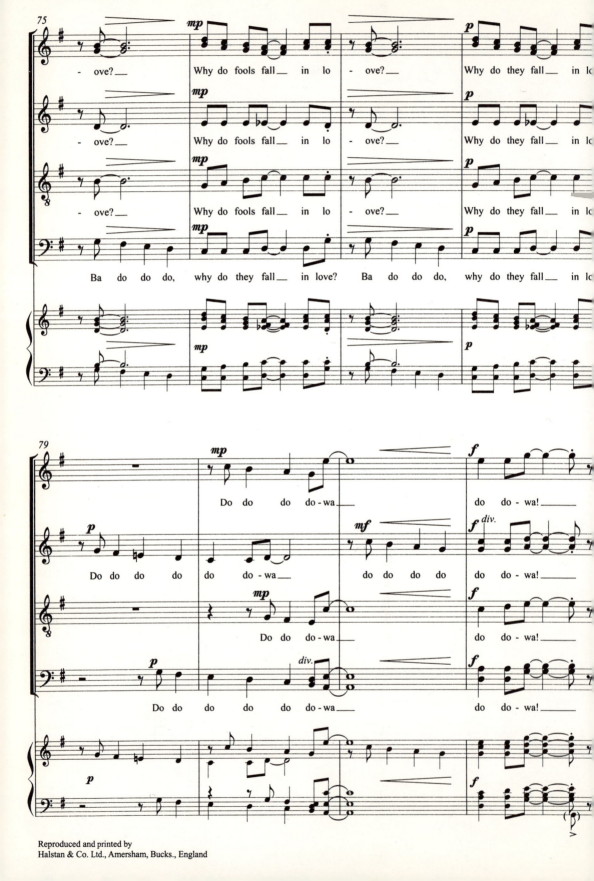